The
Power
of Love

GREAT
COMMISSION
MEDIA

Dr. Charles F. Stanley

The Power of Love

Charles Stanley
INSTITUTE FOR CHRISTIAN LIVING
Devotional Series

Published in Atlanta, Georgia, by Great Commission Media, LLC.

All Scripture quotations, unless otherwise noted, are taken from the NEW AMERICAN STANDARD BIBLE® Copyright © 1960, 1962, 1963, 1968, 1971, 1972, 1973, 1975, 1977, 1995 by The Lockman Foundation. Used by permission.

ISBN: 0-9770976-2-5

Request for information should be addressed to:
Great Commission Media
P.O. Box 548
Lebanon GA 30146

To discover other Charles Stanley teaching resources,
visit www.charlesstanleyinstitute.com or www.intouch.org

Contents

For from days of old they have not heard
or perceived by ear, nor has the eye seen
a God besides You, who acts on
behalf of the one who waits for Him.

ISAIAH 64:4

THE POWER OF LOVE

Introduction

LOVE IS ONE OF THE MOST ABUSED AND OVER-
USED WORDS IN THE ENGLISH LANGUAGE.
BUT ITS POWER IS THE ONE THING THAT WE
MOST DESPERATELY NEED.

Many people's understanding of love is based
on what Hollywood has shown them on television
or in the movies. Others only know what they
have observed in their parents' broken or troubled
marriages. Their expectations are unrealistic and
their relationships demonstrate it.

Perhaps you have been deeply hurt after you
have expressed feelings of love for someone. Deep
down we all need to be accepted and understood;
we look for meaning in others. Most of us have
experienced the pain of false love in our lives. My
goal for this book is that God will use it to help
you discover the meaning of true love and then

learn to live in its awesome power. True love is unexplainable. It is a gift from God. It originates in the spirit and carries with it the greatest power in the universe.

Sadly, there are many people who do not love anybody. They don't love themselves, they don't love God, and they don't love anything. It may be the way they grew up; perhaps they were not loved by their parents. It is likely that they have never had love demonstrated to them. They don't even know how to love. They don't know what it is. So they can't give love. Then there are those people who have genuinely loved, but they've been hurt—deeply, deeply, hurt. Painfully rejected, cast out and now alone. So in order to protect themselves, they have pulled their emotional shades down; they have built a wall around their heart. They have encircled themselves with enough self-protection so that no matter what happens, they are determined not to be hurt again. They refuse love, they shut it out, and if they sense that they are heading in that direction, they cut it off. And here is the reason—because they were deeply hurt, they are not willing to take the chance of having it happen again.

Sometimes people get married who have been deeply hurt. They are hoping that somehow the next person is going to take away all the pain. They bring into the marriage that same emotional wall that is built around their heart. They will let their spouse in, at least partially, but they will not let them in completely. Consequently, the person who married this type of person may not have realized that there was a wall. Then when disappointments come in the new relationship, they start building the wall even higher. And before long, they have shut the other person out. It does not matter what the other person does—they may continue to live together. They can have sex and not love. They can have all the rest, but until there is a genuine love, they will never have the kind of relationship that God intends for their marriage.

If you relate to any of these examples please read on carefully. If you are ever going to love, you are going to have to be vulnerable. Don't think that you can love someone, no matter who they are, and never be disappointed. Never be hurt. All of us have injured someone we love, and we have been hurt by someone who loves us. That is just part of this fallen world that we live in. But there are many people who will never experience the awesome joy and power of unconditional love because they have been hurt in the past and are not willing to be hurt again. That is why I wrote this book, to help you know and experience true love. Once you understand the fulfillment and joy of loving and being loved, you will take the chance. You will be willing to be vulnerable. I can tell you, my friend, no matter how deeply you have been wounded, no matter what they did to you, no matter how rejected, whatever it might have been; if you close the door, shut it up, build the wall, encase yourself in a type of self-imposed protection, here is what is going to happen. Love may come your way and you will miss it.

And if you miss love in your life, you have missed what life is all about.

Psychologists tell us that we can begin to alter our negative attitudes and behaviors in as little as twenty-one days if we change our habits and ways of thinking. I know that God has provided in His anointed Word everything that is needed for us to take the next step to a complete and fulfilling understanding of genuine love. I have designed this book to serve as a tool for you to use over the next thirty-one days. Read and study each of these principles, taking time to pray and meditate over every thought. The Holy Spirit will open your eyes to His truth and change your life by the power of His love.

Experiencing God's Love

We have come to know and have believed the love which God has for us. God is love, and the one who abides in love abides in God, and God abides in him. (1 John 4:16)

When I was in my late forties, a tension in my spiritual life threatened to undermine my faith. I was working hard as a pastor, but a void had developed in my heart. I preached every week and continued to practice essential spiritual disciplines, but something was definitely missing in my own soul.

I became so restless and dissatisfied that I called four of my friends— all Christian counselors—and asked them to meet with me. It was on short notice, but amazingly, they all agreed. During our first evening together, I talked for over eight hours, telling them everything about myself. After they had retired for the night, I sat alone in my room and filled seventeen legal-sized pages with the intimate details of my life.

The following morning, I poured my heart out to God and these men, revealing every piece of personal information I could think of. Still, there was no release in my spirit.

After the group reflected upon what I had said, one member asked me to talk about the death of my father—he died when I was nine months old. When I finished speaking, he said, "Charles, put your head on the table. Imagine that your father has just picked you up in his arms. What do you feel?"

An emotional dam burst precisely at that moment. I wept for a long time. In fact, I had a difficult time stopping. I wasn't sure what God was doing, but He had obviously touched the most sensitive spiritual nerve of my soul.

When I settled down, my friend asked me how I felt. "I feel warm and secure and loved," I replied and immediately began weeping again. This time, however, I realized what God was doing.

I had trusted God since I was 12 years of age. I wanted to obey God and had a little understanding of prayer and the importance of reading of God's Word. What I never truly embraced or experienced, however, was the love of God. His sweetness and loving-kindness had somehow remained a footnote in my Christian walk. That is why I seldom preached any messages on the love of Christ. How could I preach what I had not personally experienced?

Through the godly help of my friends and the tender ministry of the Holy Spirit, I was able to identify the cause of that inner void. Because my father died when I was an infant, I simply did not understand God as a loving, heavenly Father—He had been a distant, impersonal deity.

That encounter radically changed my life.

Everything took on a new purpose and meaning. My fellowship with God entered a new dimension. It was as if I started the Christian life all over again.

There may be something in your life that hinders you from fully experiencing and enjoying the most marvelous, liberating power in heaven and earth—the absolutely transforming love of God. Quiet yourself before God for a season and ask Him to make you newly aware of His love for you. Let Him use the instrument of His choosing and work in whatever way He determines.

If you do this, you will begin a fantastic new adventure with God that sweeps away the residue of the past and pours a fresh foundation for a vibrant, personal friendship with Jesus Christ, the lover of your soul.

PRAYER

God, help me to understand the depth of your love. I know in my mind that you love me; but I want to experience your love with my heart and soul, not simply read about it or examine it in a Bible study. Draw me into your love and keep me there. Amen.

JOURNAL

_____

_____

_____

_____

_____

_____

_____

_____

_____

_____

_____

_____

DAY TWO

The Father and Son

The one who does not love
does not know God, for God is love.

(1 John 4:8)

What is the strongest motivation in your life? Some people are driven by fear, greed, or lust. Others see faith as a primary incentive. But when love is present in a person's life, it is one of the most powerful motivating forces.

First Corinthians 13 is sometimes referred to as the "love chapter" of the Bible. There, the apostle Paul talks about the pre-eminence of love over knowledge, faith, generosity, and even the ultimate sacrifice of one's own life. He explains how genuine love acts—it is patient, kind, humble, polite, not jealous, not self-seeking, not provoked, keeps no record of wrongs, rejoices in truth, bears all things, believes all things, hopes all things, and never fails.

You might react to this description by thinking, *I'm not sure I can do that!* And you would be absolutely correct—no one can, in his own strength, carry out all these actions of love. It is impossible apart from almighty God, who is the source of love.

In fact, the Bible tells us God *is* love (1 John 4:8). When you trusted Jesus Christ as your personal Savior, the Holy Spirit came to live within you and, therefore, you literally have the love of God inside of you. As you surrender yourself to Him, He allows His divine love—not human love—to flow through you. That means Christians have a capacity to love that the unbeliever does not have; it surpasses what human beings can do in their own strength. The Bible terms this love "agape."

Throughout eternity, there has been a spectacular love relationship between the Father and his Son. Before the creation of the world and man, before time, Jehovah God and his only Son lived in a perfect love relationship.

After Jesus was baptized by John the Baptist, the Father in heaven expressed his delight with the Savior, announcing to all: "This is my Son, whom I love; with him I am well pleased" (Matthew 3:17). Jesus told the Jews that "the Father loves the Son and shows him all he does" (John 5:20). Speaking intimately to His disciples at the Passover Supper, Christ said plainly, "I love the Father ..." (John 14:31).

We can experience the kind of love that exists between the Father and the Son. Jesus astounded them with these words: "As the Father has loved me, so have I loved you. Now remain in my love" (John 15:9). The love of God the Father for His Son and the love of the Son for His Father are available to every Christian. God invites you through faith in His Son to share His love.

PRAYER

Lord, Thank You for the devotion of Your Son Jesus Christ. Thank You for the example He is to me of Your unfailing love. Thank You that I can know Your love in the way that He did. Help me to love You in return in a Christ-like way. Amen.

JOURNAL

Love That Heals

The LORD is near to the brokenhearted
and saves those who are crushed in Spirit.

(Psalm 34:18)

Have you ever tottered on the edge of despair, so disillusioned and disheartened that you wondered if God really loved you anymore? Have you been so wounded by painful circumstances or a loved one's careless actions that you questioned if God could really heal your hurt?

We all have experienced the anguish of such moments; and if our perspective on the love of Christ is clouded, we can succumb to spiraling depression and bitterness. How grateful I am that our Savior comes to our aid at such times with tender love.

In describing the nature of the coming Messiah's ministry, the prophet Isaiah said, "He will not cry out or raise His voice, nor make His voice heard in the street. A bruised reed He will not break, and a dimly burning wick He will not extinguish" (Isaiah 42:2-3).

More than eight hundred years later, Matthew thought of Isaiah's words and used them to describe Jesus' earthly life as He healed broken bodies and relieved tormented minds, touching the lives of physically and emotionally damaged people. Some were blind and mute, even demon-possessed. Most, no doubt, were social outcasts. But Jesus changed their dreary, desperate world into one of renewed hope and confidence. And the healing power of His love can change your world, too.

If you feel like a "bruised reed" about to break or a "dimly burning wick," take courage. The love of God is both strong and tender enough to heal your hurts and revive your spirit.

At your weakest moment, God's love is completely sufficient to sustain you. You can count on God's tender mercy to restore you in your darkest hours.

God's love is infinite and nothing can stand in its way, however great our sin or small our faith.

PRAYER

Heavenly Father, life can be difficult and, at times, I feel beaten down by adversity. I wonder where You are and if You hear my prayers—yet I know in my heart that You do. Please strengthen my faith today and renew my faith in You. Amen.

JOURNAL

Unfailing Love

We have thought on Your loving-kindness,
O God, in the midst of Your temple.

(Psalm 48:9)

I read the Psalms almost every day and each time I read them, I find a new blessing. David wrote at length about God's unfailing love, and his words of truth offer real strength and comfort.

The writers of the Old Testament used the Hebrew word *chesed* to express God's care for His children. The word—sometimes translated "loving-kindness" or "steadfast love"—conveys the permanence of God's unconditional love for us.

Unlike the love people show to one another, God's love is infinite and powerful enough to forgive the most grievous wrong. It endures life's greatest hardships and heals the deepest wounds. The steadfast love of God never changes, is never diminished by our behavior, and is never lessened by our indifference or even rebellion. Christ's love has no boundaries—it persists through all of our circumstances and through all time.

The book of Hebrews puts it this way: "Never will I leave you; never will I forsake you" (Hebrews 13:5 NIV).

Since God's love for us is unfailing and unchanging, we can rest in complete assurance of His faithfulness. King David—whose life was constantly in peril—wrote, "For the king trusts in the LORD; and through the loving kindness of the Most High he will not be shaken" (Psalm 21:7). His life was unstable at times, but his faith and trust rested securely in God's remarkable love for him—and so can ours.

If there is one thing that has stabilized my life through all these years, it is the quiet time I spend with God every morning. Moses said,

"Satisfy us in the morning with your unfailing love, that we may sing for joy and be glad all our days" (Psalm 90:14).

If you start each morning meditating on God's unfailing love, how it is expressed to you, its immensity, and its power, your life will be revolutionized. The more time you spend with the Lord, the more you will come to know His boundless love, and the more joyful you will become. The more joyful you are, the more exciting is your walk with Jesus and the more dynamic is your faith.

The steadfast love of Christ is our anchor for every storm, and what satisfies the deepest longing of our hearts.

PRAYER

Heavenly Father, I can hardly imagine what Your unfailing, unceasing love really means I do know that it is what I yearn for in my heart. Each day, grant me a more complete understanding of how much You really love me. Along the way, teach me how to express that love to those around me. Thank You for creating the need for love within me and supplying that need. Amen.

JOURNAL

_____

_____

_____

_____

_____

_____

_____

_____

_____

_____

_____

_____

_____

_____

DAY FIVE

Receiving God's Love

For His loving kindness is great toward us.
(Psalm 117:2)

One of the first verses of Scripture I learned as a young Christian—and probably the verse most believers can quote from memory—is John 3:16: "For God so loved the world, that He gave His only begotten Son, that whoever believes in Him shall not perish, but have eternal life."

As I have grown in Christ, I have come to understand that the entire Bible is the revelation of God's love for us. From Genesis to Revelation, it is the story of God's persistent desire to redeem and reconcile human beings to an eternal fellowship with Himself.

How then do we develop such stubborn resistance to receiving and enjoying God's love? Why do so many Christians live with feelings of self-condemnation, fear, and doubt? We learn of His love through the study of scripture, but the knowledge of His love often fails to resonate in our hearts. We know a great deal about sound doctrine, yet our souls yearn for His touch.

Perhaps the most obvious reason for this dilemma is the prevalence of pride in our lives. Convinced of our self-reliance, we believe we can make it on our own once God has rescued us from eternal ruin. But striving to achieve a life worthy of Christ's sacrifice without His help is an impossible endeavor that results only in exhaustion and disappointment.

Thankfully, God's powerful love can reach beyond the barriers of pride and bring us to a place of true humility. Jesus said, "Just as the Father has loved Me, I have also loved you; now abide in My love" (John 15:9). He used the Greek word *agape*, a word seldom used by the

Greeks that expresses the concept of absolute adoration.

Unconditional love means this: God loves you just the way you are. Isn't that something we all long for, to be loved without conditions or stipulations? God loves you when you obey, and He loves you when you rebel. That doesn't mean He tolerates sin—He died for it—or that He minimizes its consequences. But it does mean that His love for you is steadfast regardless of your actions.

However much you have come to depend upon yourself, it is never too late to put your faith in the Lord. When you do, His agape love will transform your life completely. He loves you as much now as He ever will, and His love comes with no strings attached—it is a free gift, given from a pure heart. This may sound too good to be true, but it isn't. Receive it, accept it, and you will never again be the same.

PRAYER

*Heavenly Father, I have relied upon myself for
so long that it is difficult to trust someone else
with my life—yet I choose to do that today. I
place my hope in You. Show me the places in my
heart where pride has taken root and help me to
surrender them to You. As I humble myself,
reveal Your words of love throughout Scripture
so I may be solidly grounded in an understanding of agape love. Amen.*

JOURNAL

_____

_____

_____

_____

_____

_____

_____

_____

_____

The Cure of Grace

We have peace with God through our Lord Jesus Christ, through whom we have gained access by faith into this grace in which we now stand.

(Romans 5:1-2)

I admit I have a "type-A" personality. I like well-defined goals, enjoy hard work, and strive to perform to the best of my ability. While there is nothing inherently wrong with this mind-set, it can sometimes lead to a self-reliance that undermines the awesome power of God's grace.

God's grace is an important reality to understand and receive. The Gospel tells us that Jesus was full of "grace and truth" (John 1:14). His message to the apostles was the triumph of grace over law. Apart from the cornerstone of grace, the gospel would be fundamentally flawed. We cannot understand Christianity or the love of Christ until we comprehend grace.

What is grace? It is God's love and kindness toward humanity without regard to the worth or merit of those who receive it, and in spite of the fact that we don't deserve it. Because of His grace, we cannot do anything to make Him love us any less or any more than He does.

When we fully grasp this reality, our tiresome efforts to perform in order to earn His love are put to rest. We don't have to be successful to be loved by God. We are redeemed only by the sacrifice of Jesus Christ, and that is a free gift for everyone willing to accept it—we can do nothing to merit it.

Unfortunately, many people are so used to earning the acceptance of their peers that they try to do the same with God. But His grace goes completely against this notion. We don't have to do anything to deserve God's affection; we are pleasing to Him because Christ died for our sin.

Are you working hard to gain God's favor? You have it. Is there always something more you think you have to do in order to be accepted? God has done all you need through the cross of Christ to make you acceptable.

Ephesians 2:8-9 tells us, "For by grace you have been saved through faith; and that not of yourselves, it is the gift of God; not as a result of works, so that no one may boast." When Paul wrote to Timothy, he encouraged the young man to find his strength in God's grace alone (2 Timothy 2:1). Christ's work on the cross has been credited to your account so you can live abundantly free from sin and guilt (John 10:10).

PRAYER

Lord, I've been plagued with feelings of guilt lately, believing I wasn't doing enough to earn your fellowship. But Romans 5 tells me I already have peace with You because of

*Your grace. I don't have to do or be anything!
Jesus Christ did it all. Thank You for that
sacrifice. Thank You for accepting me just as
I am. Amen.*

JOURNAL

_____

_____

_____

_____

_____

_____

_____

_____

_____

_____

_____

_____

_____

_____

_____

Perfect Love

This is love: not that we loved God,
but that he loved us and sent his Son as an
atoning sacrifice for our sins. (1 John 4:10)

Love is the greatest gift God offers us, and yet it
is the one we have the most difficulty receiving.
Why? First of all, we do not think we deserve
His love, which is true. Secondly, we do not
understand it—we cannot compare the quality of
God's love with our own. We somehow want to
believe that He loves us the way we love others.
However, such a viewpoint leaves us doubtful
that He will always love us as the Bible promises.

God's love is not based on emotion, as
human love often is; it is based on His character.

The Bible tells us that God is love (1John 4:8). Since it is impossible for Him to do anything contrary to His nature, His love is certain and eternal.

In addition, His love is a gift. James 1:17 teaches, "Every good and perfect gift is from above, coming down from the Father of lights, with whom there is no variation or shifting shadow." In other words, God's love is unchanging and independent of our feelings about deserving it. We cannot earn it or give anything in return for it—God's gift is something He offers freely.

Furthermore, the love of our heavenly Father is perfect. God is the absolute perfection of every aspect of His character. For example, His power is perfect power, just as His knowledge is perfect knowledge. Every one of His attributes is the peak of perfection and cannot be improved to any degree. Since His love is perfect, we know it will certainly benefit us. He will always treat us in accordance with His love.

I can remember a time when I was really

struggling with a circumstance in my life. I had become impatient, as we all do on occasion. One particular morning, I was so overwhelmed that I knelt by the bed and poured out my heart to God, asking Him, "Why don't You just get on with this?" And then it was as if God whispered to me, "You can trust perfect love." All of a sudden, my burden left, my frustration disappeared, and my anxiety vanished.

My understanding of God's love took a big step forward that day. It was suddenly clear that His love is trustworthy in any and every situation of life. Whatever you are facing, no matter how you are feeling, God is loving you . . . perfectly.

PRAYER

Dear Heavenly Father, Your love for me is perfect, and yet I so often forget that. Please help me to trust You completely—regardless of the situations I find myself in. Help me to understand Your love fully, and to put my trust in You. Amen.

JOURNAL

_____

_____

_____

_____

_____

_____

_____

_____

_____

_____

_____

_____

_____

Loving Your Enemies

But love your enemies, do good to them.
(Luke 6:35)

One of the most challenging attacks against me personally occurred early in my work at First Baptist Church of Atlanta. I had just become senior pastor after a time of controversy. As I stood in the pulpit at a meeting, one of the men approached me and struck me. That was only one of many incidents where the displeasure and anger of others were displayed.

At that moment, my emotions were strained and I had a difficult decision to make. I could respond in the flesh, or I could allow God's love to work through me. Jesus' command to love my enemies seemed nearly impossible, but I discovered the love of Christ can override our emotions and prime our will to obey.

David's awkward relationship with King Saul has helped me learn how to treat those who hurt or mistreat me. Thoroughly misunderstood and relentlessly pursued, David spent years in crags and caves while Saul enjoyed all the advantages of kingship. Twice David had opportunities to slay his tormentor. Yet he refused to exercise the option of hate, choosing instead to demonstrate his innocence and loyalty.

David did not retaliate. If we are wise, we will travel the same route. Anytime we seek revenge—subtly or blatantly—we hinder the power of God's love. Retaliation takes the matter out of God's providential hand and puts it in our sinful grasp. It violates God's law of love, which Peter defines this way: "Do not repay evil with evil or insult with insult, but with blessing" (1 Peter 3:9).

How do you not return the blow you have

received? By taking refuge in the sovereignty of God. Jesus, when hanging on a cross, "did not retaliate; when he suffered, he made no threats. Instead, he entrusted himself to him who judges justly" (1 Peter 2:23 NIV). Both David and the Messiah made God their hiding place from the schemes of wicked men, trusting Him to handle their hurts.

Entrusting yourself and your particular circumstance to God frees you to extend grace to the offending party. Love flowed from the cross. David spoke graciously and courteously to Saul. Likewise, we should do good to those who wrong us. When we speak kindly to them, the gripping thought of retaliation will fade as love takes its place.

The noblest expression of love is to give it to those who do not deserve it. That is what Jesus did when He gave Himself up for us, and aren't we called to be like Him? Love your enemies, and your faith will grow stronger. You can do it because God loved you first.

PRAYER

Lord, I admit that it is sometimes hard to love others when I am wronged by them. My natural response is to distance myself from them or somehow retaliate. I ask You to prompt my spirit to react with kindness when someone offends me. I know that I can do this only through the strength of Your Holy Spirit. Amen.

JOURNAL

The Big Picture

Man looks at the outward appearance,
but the Lord looks at the heart.

(*1 Samuel 16:7*)

We derive great inspiration from the people we read about in the Bible, but most of them were ordinary and not so different from us. Moses and Peter had very humble beginnings. David encountered serious obstacles—some of his own making—throughout his life. Gideon started slowly, fared well for a season, and ended questionably.

The common lives of these people tell us a great deal about the Christian life and our own ability to live it. Through reading the Scriptures, we can see clearly that God is equally as interested in the process of our lives as He is in the final result.

Those who trust in Christ as their Savior will arrive safely in heaven. Jesus' sacrifice on the cross settles that issue. Therefore, the process of making us more like Christ is God's primary objective during our short span on earth.

Our spiritual development involves failure and success, joy and grief, wisdom and foolishness, peace and turmoil. If you were to chart the lives of Moses and David, you would see many highs and lows. Becoming more like Christ is a lifelong endeavor that involves advancement as well as setbacks.

From the accounts recorded in Scripture, we know that God is more concerned with our progress than perfectionism. The men and women who God used historically, and the people He uses today, are far from faultless. What God does care about is a heart that is bent toward obedience to Him, repentant when wrong, contrite when disobedient, and humble when self-reliant. Although our spiritual progress includes failure, it moves us closer in our relationship with the Savior. God put up with David's failures because the King's heart was set toward Him.

Probably what impresses and encourages me most when I think about these people is this: God saw their potential for godliness and waited patiently for it to develop. What farmer discards a half-grown crop? He waters, watches, and protects it until harvest. When God saves you, He knows your tremendous spiritual potential. Peter's initial hesitation paled in comparison to his later loyalty and commitment. Moses' forty years of exile were merely preparation for forty years of tough leadership.

If you know God is interested in the process, looks for ultimate progress, and sees unlimited potential, you can be liberated to walk and act under the umbrella of His love. God's commitment is for eternity, but He is with you today to help you make the most of each opportunity. If you falter or fail, He will correct you and help you walk upright again.

PRAYER

Gracious Father, I am so grateful that You see my life from an eternal perspective and that You have a magnificent plan for my life. As much as I don't like valley experiences, it helps to know that You have not given up on me. You are so good. I just want to thank You, Lord, for having the big picture in mind. Amen.

JOURNAL

_____

_____

_____

_____

_____

_____

_____

DAY TEN

Love's Pardon

Though your sins are like scarlet,
they shall be as white as snow;
though they are red as crimson,
they shall be like wool. (Isaiah 1:18)

While working in my dark room one day, I made
an interesting discovery. I occasionally use colored
filters over my lenses when I photograph in black
and white. For instance, a light yellow filter dark-
ens the sky, while brightening the clouds. A red
filter enhances the white. That particular day,
I experimented with viewing a red dot on white
paper through a red filter. To my amazement,
the dot, when seen through the red filter,
appeared white.

This interesting find revealed to me something about the prophet Isaiah's description of sin. Our sin, depicted as deep red by Isaiah, becomes white as snow and wool when seen through the red cross of Golgotha. This is the great transformation of forgiveness. Jesus, the Lamb of God, took away our iniquity when his blood was shed on the cross. Our past sins, today's transgressions, and tomorrow's disobedience have been fully forgiven by Christ's once-and-for-all sacrifice.

By His own doing, God in Christ has cleansed you from every stain of transgression. Though you still suffer damaging consequences when you sin, you are never treated as a sinner by the Father. You are a new creation in Christ, a saint created in the image of His Son.

God's forgiveness not only takes your sins away but also credits the righteousness of Christ to your account. This is a dynamic aspect of forgiveness that is often overlooked. No blame can ever be laid to your account, because you have been justified, declared "not guilty" by the Judge Himself.

God freely expresses the fullness of His love to you because there is no barrier—justice has been satisfied. His complete forgiveness, freely given, erases all guilt. The Holy Spirit will indeed convict you of sin, but if you receive His forgiveness, you will never stand guilty before God.

This is how God sees you: pure as snow, white as wool. Your sins have been permanently cleansed through the shed blood of Christ. Since this is how He views you, shouldn't you see yourself in the same light?

PRAYER

Father, I can witness Your miracles and promises being fulfilled by simply opening my eyes to Your creation every day. Knowing that You see me as pure, whole, and blameless is a miracle in itself. I want to thank You and praise You for your perfect, living example of love. Amen.

JOURNAL

_____

_____

_____

_____

_____

_____

_____

_____

_____

_____

_____

_____

_____

_____

_____

_____

_____

_____

_____

_____

_____

_____

Experiencing God's Love

My times are in your hands.

(Psalm 31:15)

Do you sometimes wrestle with God over an issue you desperately want solved? The need is urgent, the time is short, your prayers are intense. However, God seems slow to respond. At times, there appears to be an almost inverse relationship between the magnitude of our problem and the clarity of God's response. The more we want to know His mind, the less He appears to reveal a solution.

After struggling through many long periods of waiting in my life, I have come to understand an important scriptural truth that will free us from considerable bondage and unleash God's power on our behalf. It is the principle of relinquishment.

Waiting on God's timing is one of the most profitable lessons I have ever learned. I have petitioned God on many occasions and received virtual silence as an answer. At times, the wait for a response to my prayers seemed to go on forever. But, however long He has made me wait, He has always come through in the end.

Letting go is probably one of the most difficult things that Christians are called to do. This is especially true when there is something that seems to be right at our fingertips and we think that God is about to bless us with the desire of our hearts.

By relinquishment, I do not mean resignation or passivity. I am not suggesting a mind-set of fatalism or inaction. What I do mean is letting go of a demanding spirit, quieting inner strife, and canceling our own agenda—a complete willingness to settle for God's provision.

Christ Himself is our example as He passionately communed with the Father regarding His death. "My Father, if it is possible, may this cup be taken from me. Yet not as I will, but as you will" (Matt. 26:39). Because Jesus' mission of redemption was incomplete without the cross, He had to surrender His desires to the Father: "Not my will, but Yours be done" (Luke 22:42). It was a prayer of relinquishment, arrived at only after ardent, earnest petition. When Jesus—as always—said yes to the Father, Satan's shackles of sin on mankind were shattered. The power that flowed from Calvary is the heart of the Christian faith.

When we submit to the Father's plan—whatever that may be—we release amazing power within our lives and those around us. Relinquishing a troublesome matter to God means we have placed the dilemma squarely into the hands of our Lord, whose goodness, wisdom, and power never fail.

In so doing, we trust Him completely for results. Whatever the answer, we know that it is for our best. "For I know the plans I have for you, declares the Lord, to give you a hope and a future" (Jeremiah 29:11).

PRAYER

Dear Heavenly Father, I confess that my thoughts are sometimes of base with Yours. Right now I want to give my circumstances to You. With open hands, I lay them before You, not holding on to any part of them. By faith, I am trusting You completely with my needs. Amen.

JOURNAL

_____

_____

_____

_____

_____

_____

_____

_____

No Complaints

Being confident of this, that he who began
a good work in you will carry it on
to completion until the day of Christ Jesus.

(Philippians 1:6 NIV)

Some of my fondest memories of childhood are of my mother. My father died when I was nine months old, so my mom supported the two of us for many years. She worked the swing shift at a textile mill, coming home late each night. We didn't have very many worldly possessions. In fact, we moved frequently, living in seventeen houses over a period of sixteen years.

Yet my mother seldom complained. She always expressed confidence in God to meet our needs, and she spread cheer wherever she went.

Her enthusiasm and faith were contagious.

I can't help but think of her every time I read an engaging verse of scripture tucked away in the second chapter of Philippians: "Do everything without complaining or arguing" (Philippians 2:14).

In seven concise words, Paul unveils the lifestyle that drives away bitterness, regret, and anger and promotes love. To be honest, I sometimes wonder how we can obey that command when confronted with situations that seem to bring out the worst in us.

Yet when I think of my mother and the many difficult situations she faced without a hint of murmuring, I understand her secret to a contented, thankful heart. It is not a secret really; it is a principle that every believer can practice successfully.

It is found in the verse immediately preceding Paul's command to tackle life with a hearty spirit: "For it is God who works in you to will and to act according to his good purpose" (Philippians 2:13).

We must never lose sight of the tremendous truth that God is constantly and positively at work in each detail of our lives. He is never limited by circumstances, and is never perplexed over our problems. He is actively moving in our inner being to conform us to Christ's image and is sovereignly steering events toward our good and for His glory.

We can genuinely give thanks in everything (1Thessalonians 5:16), because God is at work in all things. Why grumble or complain if God is in control and accomplishing His purposes? I am convinced that it was because my mother understood this principle that she was enabled to go about her duties with a grateful heart.

Do you see God at work in your life? If so, then each assignment of the day—great or small—bears His imprint. Refuse to yield to a critical or complaining spirit, because to do so is to actually grumble against God Himself (Exodus 16:8). But a thankful spirit promotes peace and health. It acknowledges God's love and affirms your trust in Him. It is a solid testimony to others that the God you serve is able, caring, and very wise.

PRAYER

God, forgive me for grumbling and complaining about so many things. There is much to be thankful for. I know a grateful heart promotes peace, and that is what I want. I give You permission to change my critical spirit and replace it with thanksgiving. Amen.

JOURNAL

_____

_____

_____

_____

_____

_____

_____

_____

Walking in Love

Therefore as you have received
Christ Jesus the Lord, so walk in Him"
(Colossians 2:6)

The Scriptures frequently speak about the "Christian walk" as a description of believers' behavior. For example, we are told to walk as children of light, walk in the truth, walk according to the Spirit, and walk in love. Colossians 2:6 uses this expression to give us an important command: "Therefore as you have received Christ Jesus the Lord, so walk in Him." The question we must ask is, what does it mean to "walk in Christ"?

Here, the word *in* does not have a literal

usage, like "the hammer is in the toolbox."
Rather, it refers to a vital relationship—a union
between the believer and the Lord. Just as a wed-
ding marks the beginning of a new relationship
for a man and a woman, receiving Christ as savior
commences an intimate fellowship between the
Lord and His follower. What God desires is not
simply to forgive sins, but to develop a close and
ever-deepening personal relationship with each of
His children. He wants us to realize that the Son
of God is the source of everything—Jesus Christ
is to the believer what blood is to the human
body: indispensable to life.

Therefore, "walking in Christ" refers to a
dynamic relationship with the Lord. Just as it is
impossible to walk while standing still, believers
are either moving forward in their Christian life
or falling backward. The key for how to make
progress is found in that same Colossians verse:
"As you have received Christ Jesus the Lord, so
walk in Him." How did you and I receive Christ?
By faith. In order to be born again we trusted the

testimony of the Word of God. The Christian life is to be "walked"—or lived out—in the same way.

Most people are guided by their natural senses, but that is often ineffective because, from our human viewpoint, we are unable to see the big picture. Instead, our heavenly Father wants us to trust Him daily for whatever need we may have. That is why followers of Jesus Christ are to "walk by faith, not by sight" (2 Corinthians 5:7). We must take the first step by faith, and then another, not knowing exactly where it will lead us, but trusting that our omniscient, loving God has our best interest in mind. To walk in faith means having a personal relationship with Jesus Christ that results in trusting Him for every circumstance of life. When we consistently live with that kind of confidence in the Lord, we will believe He will do what is right and what is for our benefit every time, without exception.

PRAYER

Dear Father, it is difficult to trust when the hardships of life seem so many. Yet I know that in trusting You, I will not only see the victory over adversity, but will grow closer to You. Please help me to trust You more and, in doing so, to know You more. Amen.

JOURNAL

_____

_____

_____

_____

_____

_____

_____

_____

_____

_____

_____

_____

Love's First Promise

Yet I hold this against you:
You have forsaken your first love.
(Revelation 2:4 NIV)

Is your relationship with Jesus your first priority? Have you become so preoccupied with superficial service that has all the trappings of Christianity that you don't have time for the commitment and vitality of personal fellowship?

If you have hit a plateau in your fellowship with Christ, then consider these questions: Is Jesus still "your first love"? Does spending time with the Lord still excite you? Is time spent in Scripture rewarding? Is telling others about the Savior important to you? Do you begrudge giving

God a tithe of you income? Your responses to these questions reveal much about the quality of your relationship with Jesus. Knowing Him as your first love means you are increasingly excited about His character, His ways, and His Word.

Activity, though essential to practical faith, is not a substitute for personal fellowship. It can never outweigh intimacy with God. It is actually possible to become so busy "serving God" that our primary focus is taken off the Messiah and placed on other things—and that is the beginning of idolatry.

The gods of this age—sports, work, money, sex—while not bad in and of themselves, can too often become substitutes for our devotion to God. If something—regardless of what it is—distracts you from fellowship with Christ, it can soon become an idol.

How can you recapture that first love? Remember what Christ did for you when you were saved: the supernatural transformation that took you from death to life, from darkness to

light, from the dominion of sin to the reign of
Christ. Repent of whatever has diminished your
love for Jesus. Turn away from that which distracts you. Spend time in prayer and study with
the single purpose of encountering God—listening, worshiping, and obeying.

As a young Christian, I was introduced to the
writings of Oswald Chambers, who put his relationship with Christ above all else. In his book
The Moral Foundations of Life, Chambers wrote,
"Never allow anything to fuss your relationship to
Jesus Christ, neither Christian work, nor Christian
blessing, nor Christian anything. Jesus Christ first,
second, and third, and God himself by the great
indwelling power of the Spirit within will meet
the strenuous effort on your part and slowly and
surely you will form the mind of Christ and
become one with him as he was one with the
Father."

PRAYER

Dear Lord, it's easy to take Your love for grant-ed, to become so preoccupied with the business of everyday life that we spend less and less time with You. Yet our fellowship with You is the most important time we spend each day. Please help me to place You first in my life and to guard my sacred time with You. Amen.

JOURNAL

An Encouraging Word

[Paul] traveled through that area, speaking many words of encouragement to the people.
(Acts 20:2 NIV)

Have you ever been healed or inspired by the encouraging words of a close friend? I can still remember a time long ago when this happened to me—I was only six years old. On that memorable day, as I was leaving my school room, I overheard my teacher comment to another, "I like Charles." It was the first time a person other than my mom had ever said they liked me. I was touched. Her three simple words were emotional fuel that boosted my confidence and even changed the way I viewed myself.

Have you ever thought how influential your words are? Do you know what kind of impact your speech can have on a person who desperately needs to hear an encouraging word? Solomon wrote, "Pleasant words are a honeycomb, sweet to the soul and healing to the bones" (Proverbs 16:24). What a wonderful way to describe our conversation. It can be medicine to a weary soul, healing to a bruised spirit. Kind words, spoken in due season, are God's bridges of love.

If you've been on the receiving end of gracious comments, you know the power of well-chosen words. Perhaps a coach noticed you at practice one day and remarked how well you had performed. Or maybe a co-worker came to you and commended your work and attitude on a difficult task. Paul describes such speech as being "full of grace, seasoned with salt" (Colossians 4:6). Our remarks, he says, are to be flavored with gentleness and lovingkindness, key ingredients of grace-filled speech.

The love of Christ can transform our speech if we allow Him to work in our life. When your words reflect the His love and compassion, you will see a profound change in your relationships.

Ask God to make you aware of the needs of others. When we are completely absorbed in our own problems or activities, complimentary words rarely grace our conversation. But when our focus is on edification, rather than condemnation, our speech can be used for "building others up according to their needs, that it may benefit those who listen" (Ephesians 4:29 NIV).

PRAYER

Heavenly Father, speak through me words of encouragement. Help me to take my focus off of my own problems and make me sensitive to the needs of others. Amen.

JOURNAL

_____

_____

_____

_____

_____

_____

_____

_____

_____

_____

_____

_____

_____

_____

_____

_____

_____

_____

_____

_____

_____

_____

_____

Our Greatest Privilege

May the Lord direct your hearts into God's love.

(2 Thessalonians 3:5)

Of all the people you have met, whom do you feel most privileged to know? Is it an athlete or accomplished performer? Perhaps it is an admired co-worker, precious grandparent, or godly friend. As special as such people might be, our supreme privilege is to know God.

A personal relationship with the Sovereign Lord of the universe is an unparalleled opportunity and eternal treasure. Nothing else in human existence—no experience, friendship, or knowledge—can bring you lasting peace, joy, fulfillment, or security. Nothing else can offer eternal life.

The apostle Paul recognized that even the
most highly esteemed achievements pale in comparison to the "surpassing value of knowing
Christ" (Philippians 3:7-8). His consuming desire
was to know the God who had transformed his
very being. In contrast, many people go through
life without ever knowing Him. They reach the
end of their days as unbelievers, having failed to
discover the purpose for which they were created
and missing the blessings God had in store. This
is a great tragedy!

Why do people fail to know their Creator?
To begin with, many individuals live in darkness,
unaware that there is one true God whom the
Lord Jesus Christ came to reveal. Perhaps they
were never exposed to Christian truths which,
unfortunately, is common even inside the walls
of many churches.

Another reason is the lack of interest in God.
With cell phones, radios, televisions, and comput-
ers, we are overwhelmed with information, but
no wiser than we were without them. Convinced

that access to information equals knowledge, we often replace true wisdom with trivia. Even if diplomas cover your walls, unless you know Jesus Christ as your personal Savior, you are ignorant about the most important thing in life—you cannot know God without knowing Christ (John 14:7).

Finally, knowing God includes a cost, and some people are simply unwilling to pay the price. Too often, once people get saved, they become satisfied—they are not interested in investing time in Scripture and prayer to know the Father more deeply. For any relationship to grow, we must spend time communicating, listening, and making an effort to understand more about the other person.

Do you really want to know God? The way to do that is by knowing Christ: receive Him as your Savior, who paid your sin-debt in full. Then accept His invitation to spend time in private conversation—He wants your undivided attention for a little while.

PRAYER

Lord, I do love You. I may not know exactly how to express my love, but I know I can count on You to instruct me through your Word. I ask, Lord, that You will supernaturally empower me to love others as Christ loves them. Guard my intentions, that they will not be misunderstood. Let others see Jesus, not me. Amen.

JOURNAL

Love in Action

Let us … love with actions and in truth.

(1 John 3:18 NIV)

He was my Sunday school teacher, and a good one. But I remember him for something else. Craig Stowe would stop me on the street while I was on my paper route and purchase a newspaper. He would spend five or ten minutes chatting, asking me about my family, school, and things that matter to a young boy. Not only that, he always gave me more than what the newspaper cost. It didn't take me long to figure out that Craig Stowe didn't need to buy a newspaper—he got the newspaper at home.

What that man did each week for several

years demonstrated God's love to me. He went out of his way to show that he wasn't just my Sunday school teacher. He involved himself in my life in a tangible way, and I will never forget him.

Kind words are important, as we know, but kind deeds exhibit the love of Christ in a tangible way. Jesus didn't just say He loved us; He demonstrated His love by dying for our sin. (Romans 5:8) Only hours before He was to die, Jesus told His disciples that the world would know they were His followers by their love for each other (John 13:35). He obviously meant they would live in a way that visibly and practically expressed God's love.

Barnabas encouraged a downcast young man named Mark who later penned one of the gospels. Mary and Martha showed their love for Christ by inviting him to dine and rest in their home in Bethany. Paul reminded Titus that Christ's death not only saved us from sin but should motivate us to be "eager to do what is good" (Titus 2:14). We were "created in Christ

Jesus to do good works" (Ephesians 2:10).

By doing for others in the spirit of our biblical ancestors, we can proclaim the gospel without saying a word: bake a pie for a busy mother, mow the yard for the elderly neighbor, invite a lonely person from the Sunday school class out to lunch, take time for a coffee break with that frustrated co-worker, help the new neighbor unload the boxes that are still in his garage, or write an encouraging note to someone struggling to adapt to new surroundings.

Sharing God's love in this manner personifies the compassion of Christ and says, "I care" louder than any words possibly could. All it takes is a willing spirit to lift another believer. Nothing but good comes from doing good.

PRAYER

Lord, I've been a little selfish with my idle time lately. I worry about my own problems so much that I forget that others around me have needs as well. Show me how to demonstrate Your concern to others around me. Thank You for the many times others have gone out of their way to show me special attention. Their actions have always been a boost when I've been down. Amen.

JOURNAL

When We Praise

*I will...praise your name for your love
and your faithfulness.*

(Psalm 138:2 NIV)

The more you love God, the more you will worship Him. Love and praise are natural partners. Heaven is a place where those who love God live in constant praise of Him. Should your present experience be any different?

We praise God for what He has done. "Praise him for his acts of power," writes the Psalmist in Psalm 150:2. His "acts of power" are the extraordinary events recorded in Scripture—creation, miracles, the cross, the resurrection. They also are the remarkable displays of His per-

sonal love for you. Why not write down some of
the ways that God has demonstrated His power
in your life? Think of His guidance, His provision, His protection, and the numerous other
ways He has supplied your personal needs. A
journal that records God's handiwork in your life
is a tremendous tool for joyful praise.

We praise God for "His surpassing greatness"
(Psalm 150:2). This is pure praise, standing in
awe of God for who He is. He is faithful, kind,
good, just, holy, patient and generous. God acts
greatly because he is a great God. His character
and attributes should overwhelm us. Our
response should be nothing short of ecstatic
gratitude. Think of this: you have the opportunity to praise a personal, perfect God who takes
great interest in who you are and what you do.

Praise magnifies God and puts problems into
perspective. What obstacle is too big for God?
What circumstance is too difficult for Him? Many
times I have come to God with a consuming burden, only to find it has been lifted after a session

of praise and worship.

Praise reveals our devotion to Christ. Habakkuk the prophet wrote that he would praise God even in the worst of times, when the "olive crop fails and the fields produce no food, though there are no sheep in the pen and no cattle in the stalls" (Habakkuk 3:17). Even if you are caught in such a worst-case scenario, God still deserves your praise. From experience, I can tell you that praise is the one factor that will deliver you from the sinkhole of depression and discouragement.

Express your love for Christ by making praise a priority. Enter His presence with a thankful heart before you present your request, and choose to praise in difficult times—it makes all the difference.

PRAYER

Heavenly Father, I do want to praise You. I do not want to dwell on my problems and needs, but only on all You have done for me. Your Word tells me that from the very beginning of time, You had a plan for my life, desiring for me to accept Your Son as my Savior. You have watched over me, and directed my life for my good and Your glory. Thank You for all You have done for me. Amen.

JOURNAL

_____

_____

_____

_____

_____

_____

_____

_____

_____

Love is More Than a Feeling

No one can snatch them out of my hand.

(John 10:28)

Sir Winston Churchill once remarked that it was dangerous to "always [be] feeling one's pulse and taking one's temperature." His words were addressed to those who looked at the wildly fluctuating fortunes of battles to determine England's success or failure in World War II.

His words are applicable to the Christian who constantly gauges his relationship with Christ by his feeling. Emotions are unreliable barometers, and if you attach your faith to them, you will, without a doubt, be misguided. Certainly, we are to love God and do things that please Him, such as reading His Word, spending time in prayer, and joining with a local body of believers. But there are times when the Bible seems cold, our prayers listless, our commitment to the church uncertain; and if we allow our feelings to govern our fellowship with Christ in these instances, we are sure to drift into guilt and self-condemnation.

The Bible tells us to "love the Lord our God with all our heart, soul, and mind" (Luke 10:27). We do this not by working up enthusiasm for Him, but by understanding the incredible depth of His love for us. The prescription for a steady, progressive walk of faith is focusing on God rather than ourselves. His love is unchanging and fixed forever.

Think about this illustration: Imagine your hand and God's clasped together. Your grip loosens during a season of temptation, sin, doubt, or apathy. Your feelings of love for God are minimal. But rather than focusing on your hand, you look to the hand of God. His grip of love is solid.

He will not let go. "Your right hand upholds me," declared David from the deserts of Judah (Psalm 63:8). "For I am the Lord, your God, who takes hold of your right hand," said God to a fearful people (Isaiah 41:13).

You are eternally secure in the love of God. You are sealed by the Holy Spirit, and Heaven awaits you. In this light, you can cease—as Churchill said—exercising self-centered faith. You can stop measuring the depth of your love for Christ by inconsistent feelings, and instead base them on the unwavering love of God.

PRAYER

Heavenly Father, I can be so easily influenced by my feelings, and the results of my actions can be devastating. Strengthen my faith in You. My heart's desire is to grasp Your hand firmly at all times. Teach me to overcome feelings that are damaging to my faith. Thank You, Father, for Your steadfast love. Amen.

JOURNAL

True Love Gives

For God loves a cheerful giver.

(2 Corinthians 9:7)

When I consider a scriptural synonym for love, I am drawn to the constant biblical use of the word *give*. "For God so loved the world that He gave His one and only Son . . . " (John 3:16). "I live by faith in the Son of God, who loved me and gave Himself for me" (Galatians 2:20).

God gives you the gift of salvation and the Holy Spirit. He gives peace, strength, and wisdom to those who ask.

It is impossible to love someone without giving. We bestow our affection on family members and friends with various forms of giving.

We demonstrate our commitment to Christ and others by giving our time, our resources, and our energies. Generosity is a true hallmark of genuine Christianity. Proverbs 11:25 (NIV) tells us, "A generous man will prosper; he who refreshes others will himself be refreshed." Giving is the channel through which the love of God flows.

You may think you have too little to give, but whatever your financial or physical situation, there is always something you can offer others. If you wait until you have a surplus to give, you will never begin. A generous person demonstrates God's love by giving even the little things—a listening ear, a tip for the grocery boy, a handmade gift for Christmas.

Have you ever noticed that people are drawn to a generous person, not for a handout, but because of the inviting spiritual atmosphere that surrounds him? A generous person is sensitive to the needs of others and gives from the heart, not for the purpose of receiving something in return. He derives joy in seeing others benefit from his benevolence. He views needs as an opportunity, not a threat. He wants to see how much he can give, not how little. He trusts God for his own needs.

Why is giving so important? Because it is the certain cure for greed. God blesses generosity and curses greed. Giving is the antidote for selfishness, a lifestyle that does not reflect the likeness of Christ. Generosity also opens the heart of both giver and receiver to the love of Christ. Both can become spiritually prosperous by exercising the important principle of giving.

If you are reluctant to give, stingy with your resources, and isolated from the needs of others, you are missing out on fantastic blessings from your generous heavenly Father. "Give and it will be given to you," Jesus promised (Luke 6:38). Such is the power of generosity. Give something today and watch God work.

PRAYER

Dear Jesus, giving any amount or any thing appears sacrificial at this point. But I have read Your words and listened to the testimonies of others that reveal the blessings of heartfelt giving. Today, show me a way that I can give of myself to benefit others and glorify You. Amen.

JOURNAL

_____

_____

_____

_____

_____

_____

_____

_____

_____

_____

_____

Willing to Say Yes

For Christ's love compels us.

(2 Corinthians 5:14 NIV)

The Lord's simple requests are often stepping-stones to life's most wonderful blessings. Simon Peter is a good illustration of what happens when we say yes to God. In Luke 5:1-11, people were pressing in around Jesus while He was preaching. The Lord wanted to use Peter's boat as a floating platform from which to address the crowd on shore, so He asked the future apostle to push the vessel out a little way (v.3). This in itself was not a particularly remarkable request, but Peter's compliance paved the way for multiple blessings. From his example, we learn how essential it is to obey God in even the smallest matters.

Immediately, the crowd was blessed by Peter's obedience—they were now able to hear Jesus' words as He taught. Then, when the lesson was completed, the Lord said to Peter, "Put out into the deep water and let down your nets for a catch" (v. 4) Here was another opportunity to say yes or no, and Peter must have felt tempted not to consent. After all, he had worked the entire night in hopes of a catch but had returned empty-handed. And now Jesus was telling him to go fishing again! But notice what happened as a result of Peter's obedience: on a day that he and his colleagues had written off as a total loss, they pulled in not one, but two overflowing boatloads of fish (v.7). Saying yes to the Lord's request resulted in a miracle that absolutely transformed the fisherman's life.

Obedience is critical to the successful Christian life, and obeying God in small matters is an essential step to receiving God's greatest blessings. Suppose Peter had said, "I'm busy cleaning my nets right now. I can't help you because I'm going fishing again tonight—I just don't have time." Or he could have said, "Why don't you ask to use that other boat over there?" or "I've already been fishing today. It would be a waste of time to go again right now." Peter could have said a number of things. If he had said anything other than yes, he would have missed the greatest fishing experience of his life. But because of Peter's obedience, the Lord arranged a miracle he would never forget.

Oftentimes God's greatest blessings come as a result of our willingness to do something that appears to be very insignificant. Has God been challenging you to do something seemingly unimportant that you have not yet made an effort to accomplish? Is there anything you have rationalized by saying, "It's too difficult," "I don't want to," or "I have to pray about it"? Obey God today and receive His full blessing.

PRAYER

Dear God, it is easy to serve you out of a sense of duty, rather than love. I love you, Lord, because You first loved me. I want to serve you not from a place of fear, but out of love and devotion. Help me to discern the difference so I may be used effectively by you. Amen.

JOURNAL

_____

_____

_____

_____

_____

_____

_____

_____

_____

_____

_____

Our Father's Love

For great is your love toward me.

(Psalm 86:13 NIV)

When you pray, by what name do you address God? While all of the grand titles we have given Him are appropriate, as Christians we have the awesome privilege of calling God "Father." We can also *know* Him that way.

The possibility of having such a relationship with God was a revolutionary concept in the first century (Matthew 6:9). The Old Testament contains only fifteen references to God as "Father," and those speak primarily of Him as the Father of the Hebrew people; the idea of Him being a personal God to individuals is not evident until the

New Testament. Yet that is the reason Jesus Christ came to earth—to die on the cross for our sins and reveal the heavenly Father so that you and I might know Him intimately.

"Father," which appears 245 times in the New Testament, was Jesus' favorite term for God—He spoke it fourteen times just in the Sermon on the Mount and also used this name to begin prayer (Matthew 5-7). The Lord's purpose was to reveal that God is not merely a transcendent force somewhere in the universe, but rather a loving, personal, heavenly Father who is profoundly interested in the details of our life.

Most people, including believers, do not think of God as being close like a parent, especially if they are living in disobedience. Yet Scripture repeatedly refers to Him as "Father." Paul's letters, for example, begin that way, and the apostle describes believers as the household or family of God—he calls them God's children and fellow heirs with His Son Jesus Christ. (Romans 8:17)

The privilege of knowing God as Father involves more than acquaintance with Him as a person or spirit; it goes far beyond simple familiarity with His matchless grace, love, and kindness, and even surpasses knowing Him in His holiness, righteousness, and justice. How wonderful that we—mere creations—are able to know Him personally as our very own heavenly parent. By addressing Him as "Father," Jesus revealed His intention that we understand what the saints of the Old Testament could not fully grasp: we can have the blessing of intimate kinship with the living God of the universe. In fact, it is through the person of Jesus Christ that we are able to know God in this way.

Do you know God as your heavenly Father? If not, realize that He stands ready to adopt you into His family. (Galatians 3:26) All it takes is trusting Jesus Christ as your personal Savior. John 1:12 says, "As many as received Him, to them He gave the right to become children of God, even to those who believe in His name."

PRAYER

Dear Jesus, it's good to know I have such an intimate friend as You. Because of Your omnipotence, I can trust You to lead me through the dark shadows of life. I know You will always be right beside me. Thank you, dear Friend. Amen.

JOURNAL

Love's Promise

There is no fear in love.
But perfect love drives out fear.
(1 John 4:18)

Doctors, psychologists, and counselors tell us that one of the things people want most is to be accepted, and that most will go to great lengths to gain approval. The result has left us fighting an intense battle with loneliness and fear—fear that no one will love us, and loneliness from the isolation that comes from striving after something we were never created to seek.

When we struggle for the approval of others, we disregard the unconditional acceptance of God. Essentially, we tell Him His love is not good enough and we need the regard of others first. Jesus told His disciples to seek the kingdom of God first and all their needs would be met (Matthew 6:33).

When the focus of our heart is placed squarely on God, every need, every desire we may have is fulfilled. The result of a right relationship with God is an abiding peace that comes from His presence within us through the power of the Holy Spirit. God loves you regardless of the bumps, bruises, and emotional scars you have collected over the years. He cares when you hurt and when you suffer discouragement. He is your eternal friend. Only God has the capacity to show such incredible love and acceptance.

Jesus took great care to assure His disciples that His impending death was not the end of God's presence on earth. A comforter, one who possessed the same characteristics as He did, would come. Jesus said, "I will ask the Father, and He will give you another Helper . . . that is the Spirit of truth, whom the world cannot receive, because it does not see Him or know Him, but you know Him because He abides with you, and will be in you. I will not leave you as orphans; I will come to you" (John 14:16-18).

Wise relationships always require some type of communication. Jesus made an eternal pledge to us when He came to earth. For us to realize the completeness of God's fellowship, we, too, must make a commitment to Him.

The essence of the Christian life does not consist of a set of rules and regulations. It is sharing a moment-by-moment, intimate relationship with the Savior. It is not a matter of human acceptance. God accepts us—that is all we need.

Friendship with the Savior is a continuous unveiling of His love and personal care for each of us. The life that remains focused on Jesus Christ is a life that enjoys unbroken fellowship. It is a life of victory, peace, hope, security, and, most of all, friendship.

PRAYER

Dear heavenly Father, Your love is never-ending and Your protection is always present. Please help me to focus on the love of Christ as I go through my day, and cause that love to spill over into my other relationships. Amen.

JOURNAL

_____

_____

_____

_____

_____

_____

_____

_____

_____

_____

_____

_____

_____

Tough Love

Those whom I love I rebuke and discipline.

(Revelation 3:19 NIV)

Cloth can be used to dust off a piece of gold, but for embedded impurities to be removed, the metal has to be refined. In other words, it must be melted by fire so that any tarnish or flaw can rise and be skimmed from the surface.

The Christian life is often compared to this process (Malachi 3:3). When we face struggles, God is refining us like precious metal, digging deep into our lives to eliminate all the dirt and impurities. He does this not to hurt us, but rather to help us grow into beautiful reflections of His Son.

David met the stern love of God on several occasions for his waywardness. The psalmist learned that God rebuked him harshly when necessary. Peter felt the sting of God's tough love as he denied Christ. Paul had harsh words for Mark after the young disciple wandered away on his first missionary journey. Eventually, we all discover that God is serious about the business of holiness; and when hard actions are called for, He will oblige.

Perhaps you have enforced strict guidelines with a strong-willed child. Or you have had to make some hard decisions at work regarding problem employees. Whatever the circumstance, love sometimes must be expressed in stern tones in order to be effective.

God's discipline, however, is always motivated by love. "The Lord disciplines those he loves" (Hebrews 12:6). Don't fall into self-pity when God corrects you. This is actually a reminder that He cares for you enough to keep you from self-destructing. God only disciplines, never condemns us.

The context of God's discipline is a father/child relationship. "Endure hardship as discipline; God is treating you as sons" (Hebrews 12:7). You are not a stranger to God. You are His child and, as such, you experience His fatherly correction. Do not mistake God's discipline for anger and feel that your relationship with Him has cruelly changed when adversity strikes. You have been adopted into His family, and discipline only enables you to fully enjoy the benefits of His fatherhood.

Never forget that God disciplines us for our good, that we may share in his holiness (Hebrews 12:10). The pain of chastisement has a purpose—to conform us to the image of Jesus Christ. Therefore, do not turn away or become bitter when God's sternness is directed toward you. It is a sign of His love, and the goal is to remove impediments and strengthen you for life's journey.

PRAYER

My loving Father, the struggles of this life are difficult and hard to understand. Yet I know that as I endure each trial, You are there with me. Furthermore, I know that You have a purpose in every hardship. As much as I don't like to be disciplined, I am very grateful that You love me enough to intervene in my life in such a way. Amen.

JOURNAL

Faithful Promises

He has given us his very great
and precious promises.

(2 Peter 1:4 NIV)

At a crucial time in my life, when the church I pastored faced an overwhelming obstacle, God strengthened my faith with this verse of Scripture: "You are the God who performs miracles; you display your power among the peoples" (Psalm 77:14 NIV). I meditated on that verse daily, applying it to the problem at hand. I wasn't sure of the outcome, but I was sure of the promise. Faithfully, God intervened and blessed the congregation with a supernatural answer.

You, too, can rely on the promises of God's

Word. The Bible is a book of principles as well as promises. It is full of verses that teach us of God's intention to graciously bestow good gifts. Some promises are conditional; God will act in a certain way if you obey a certain command, as in, "Give, and it will be given to you" (Luke 6:38). But there are thousands of scriptures that wait only for a ready faith and a willing spirit to claim them.

Bible promises are assertions of God's love for you. God has assumed full responsibility for meeting your needs and provides promises as one means of His supply. You can claim promises from Him that apply to all your needs. If anxiety plagues you, Philippians 4:6-7 and Psalm 46:10 are God's answers. You can be certain that God will fulfill all of His promises, but you must learn patience. He operates according to His time schedule, not yours. He sees the end from the beginning and knows precisely when to act. Don't lose heart or be discouraged in the process. It may take days, months, even years for the promise to bear fruit, but God will keep His word. Remain focused on God's Word, letting Him speak to you specifically through the Scriptures. Be obedient in your daily trials, yielded and submitted to the revealed will of God.

God's promises are anchors for your soul. They keep you grounded in His love and faithfulness, reminding you of your dependence on Him. What God promises, He will fulfill. As David Livingstone, the noted missionary, said, "It is the word of a Gentleman of the most sacred and strictest honour, and there's an end on it!" Claim it as your own, and stand in faith until God replies.

PRAYER

Thank You, Lord, for standing behind Your promises. They are reliable and trustworthy and for me. Your Word is truth, and I can always count on that when the need is great. Help me to learn Your promises that apply to my circumstances and to stand firmly in You. Amen.

JOURNAL

_____

_____

_____

_____

_____

_____

_____

_____

_____

_____

_____

_____

_____

_____

_____

_____

_____

_____

_____

_____

_____

_____

_____

DAY TWENTY-SIX

Waiting on the Lord

So Jacob served seven years to get Rachel,
but they seemed like only a few days
to him because of his love for her.
(Genesis 29:20)

It can take an entire day for me to capture the image I want for a photograph. Waiting for the right light, framing the shot exactly, properly checking for the right exposure, etc. But those outings seldom seem long or tedious to me because I love photography. Time flies when you are having fun—when you love what you are doing and are excited about the results.

Do you love what you do, or are you more likely to complain? Is your heart content, "having the continual feast of happiness" that Proverbs describes (Proverbs 15:15), or is it weighed down with anxiety or boredom? Regardless of the sadness or monotony of your surroundings, God can transform your attitude so you can approach your tasks and relationships with a cheerful disposition.

Jim Elliot, the missionary who was martyred in Ecuador, said, "Wherever you are, be all there." You may want to be in another job, another marriage, another state, or another home; but the key to enjoying life is contentment with your present lot, as difficult as that may be. "Godliness actually is a means of great gain when accompanied by contentment" (1 Timothy 6:6). It is good to dream and set goals, but focus your energy on making the most of where God has placed you.

The author of Ecclesiastes tells us, "that every man who eats and drinks sees good in all his labor—it is the gift of God" (Ecclesiastes 3:13). Your life is a gift from God, whatever your situation. Even in strenuous seasons, we can discover deep inner peace through knowing

Christ. When you face the drudgery of hardship, remember that God has orchestrated your life according to His perfect will. Your circumstances may not always be wrapped in pretty packages, but the loving hand of God—for your good—gives them. The joy of the Lord really can become your strength.

With God's help, you can learn to love what you do, enjoy being where you are, and be satisfied with your relationships. When that happens, then—as with Jacob—the years will seem like only a few days, and your joy will be full.

PRAYER

Dear Father, You know I have been unhappy in my current situation. I've been guilty of looking at others' lives, wanting what they have, not what I have. I want to make a change right now. I need Your help in changing my attitude. Instill within me a happy, cheerful outlook in all that I do and an understanding that this is Your will for my life now. Amen.

JOURNAL

_____

_____

_____

_____

_____

_____

_____

_____

_____

_____

_____

_____

_____

_____

_____

_____

_____

_____

_____

_____

_____

_____

_____

_____

A Lifetime Impact

*God our Savior…wants all men to be saved
and to come to a knowledge of the truth.*

(1 Timothy 2:3-4)

Every one of us has the potential to influence
other people. One way we do this is by purpose-
ful impact. For example, to raise godly children,
parents specifically instruct them about the
reliability of scripture, reverence for God, and
the priority of obedience to Him. In this way,
biblical truths are intentionally imparted to the
next generation. There is also a second way—
passive influence—whereby a person simply puts
faith into practice in front of others.

While my mother impacted me in both ways,

her passive influence was so compelling that I would never have considered being disobedient to God or neglecting to fulfill His purpose for my life. She had only a sixth grade education, so it was not a vast storehouse of knowledge, but rather what I saw and felt, that impacted me forever. I observed my mother obediently living out her faith, even when she had nothing, and her witness profoundly affected me. From my early childhood until I left home, my mother knelt by my bed and prayed with and for me. I learned to pray, not by her explanations, but by feeling her presence next to me and hearing her call my name before God.

If you truly want to impact your children to live a godly life, live a godly life before them. Take the time to influence your family deliberately, teaching them biblical truths and principles. But also demonstrate those principles in your own life. Children will never forget the way you handled yourself in the midst of adversity, how you showed others respect, or the manner in which you prayed. The things that impact your life will impact theirs. When children see you giving generously, do you think they will forget? Can they fail to recall that they heard you talking about your love and concern for other people, or that they saw you weep with compassion over someone else's heartaches and difficulties?

This same principle holds true with co-workers and acquaintances. As they observe your behavior, your life will influence theirs, either for good or evil. Therefore, be certain your life is pure and bright, so it will make a positive impact.

PRAYER

Lord, when I think back, I remember that it was the demonstration of Your love through someone else that made me yearn for You. I want to have that same impact on others. Live Your life through me, and let my conversation, conduct, and character reflect You. Amen.

JOURNAL

Forgiveness

Be kind and compassionate to one another, . . .
just as in Christ God forgave you.
(Ephesians 4:32 NIV)

It was a memorable dinner—not for the food, but
for the conversation. In the dining room of our
home, God was righting some wrongs between
my children and me. I wanted to know if there
was any unforgiveness in their hearts toward me,
or if while rearing them, I had done something
that deeply hurt them.

My son spoke first, "Dad, do you remember
the time you were in your study and I was prac-
ticing my music? I had played the same part many
times over and I admit it was very loud. You

came into the living room and said, 'Is that all you know?' As far as I was concerned, you were rejecting both me and my music. That hurt." Then my daughter spoke up, "When I was five years old and we lived in Miami, you sent me to my room and made me stay there for the rest of the night. I cried and cried."

They shared other instances when they felt I had offended them. Now, I could have defended myself, but I knew there was only one thing I should do—ask them to forgive me. They did, and the air of resentment was cleared.

Whether you have wronged a person or a person has wronged you, forgiveness is the only viable option to fully experience the love of God. When you seek forgiveness or extend it, you launch Christ-like love into the heart of the problem. An unforgiving spirit is poison. It stagnates Christian growth, pollutes your relationship with Jesus, and robs you of personal joy. A forgiving spirit hurdles emotional barriers and heals spiritual scars.

Start the healing process by first examining yourself and repenting of an unforgiving spirit. Thomas a Kempis wrote, "We carefully count others' offenses against us, but we rarely consider what others may suffer because of us." Continue the healing process by canceling the debt of wrongs against you. The process is emotionally charged, but it is a matter of choice, not feelings. This releases the person from your judgment just as God released you from sin's debt when He forgave you. Recognize that your offender has exposed an unforgiving attitude in you that God can heal when you choose to pardon.

All time spent in the mire of an unforgiving spirit is wasted time. It counts for nothing, and advances nothing. But the moment you forgive, the restoration process begins. Bitterness loses its hostile grip, and the freedom of forgiveness is ushered in. You can never be fully free until you fully forgive.

PRAYER

Lord, it's incredible how past unresolved hurts can affect so much of our lives. I do not want anything to come between me and the love You have to give. I know there are hurts I must deal with and correct. Please bring to my mind those past wrongs and give me the wisdom to make them right. Amen.

JOURNAL

_____

_____

_____

_____

_____

_____

_____

_____

_____

_____

Solving Problems Through Prayer

I love the LORD, for he heard my voice;
he heard my cry for mercy. Because he turned
his ear to me I will call on him as long as I live.
(Psalm 116:1-2 NIV)

Two things are said to be certain—death and taxes. Let me add a third—problems. But unlike the first two, you can do something about the latter. You can pray. In His love, God has provided prayer as a means for us to fellowship with Him and access His wisdom for our problems. God is in the problem-solving business, and when you present your dilemmas to Him, He will answer.

His reply may, or may not, be what you thought or wanted, and it may not fit neatly into your schedule. Nonetheless, God has entered into a covenant relationship with you whereby He assumes the awesome responsibility to help you, lead you, correct you, and make His will known to you. Prayer is the means of allowing Him to help you.

Present your problem to God. We don't have to be afraid of being transparent before God—He already knows what is bothering us. David poured his heart out to God, and learned to trust Him in the process—we can, too. The more specific you are in prayer, the more readily you can discern His answer.

Expect God to act. God told His people to call on Him and watch Him do great things (Jeremiah 33:3). Your petitions are meaningless if you do not anticipate God's response. That is what faith is about—seeing Him moving and working behind our natural circumstances. Wait for the Lord's reply and remember that your problem awaits *His* solutions, not yours. In his essay "The Efficacy of Prayer," C. S. Lewis wrote, "If an infinitely wise Being listens to the request of finite and foolish creatures, of course He will sometimes grant and sometimes refuse them." God's solutions are always best, even if they do not align with our desires.

Thank God during the interval. Thanksgiving acknowledges God's faithfulness and love when circumstances say otherwise. A thankful heart rejoices in the God who answers, as much as it does in the answer itself.

God is greater than your problem and is eminently able to resolve it. The power of prayer can never be overestimated because of the omnipotent God who hears and answers. Be willing to work out your difficulty His way, follow His instructions, and assume the risk that He may or may not remove the problem. In any case, your petitions will set the stage for the best possible solution when you put your trust in the God who cares.

PRAYER

Dear Father in Heaven, Thank You for the gift of prayer. That I can talk with You personally and that You listen to my petitions is nothing less than a miracle. Teach me how to better communicate with You, and to trust You fully. Amen.

JOURNAL

_____

_____

_____

_____

_____

_____

_____

_____

_____

_____

_____

_____

Tested and True

For our light and momentary troubles
are achieving for us an eternal glory
that far outweighs them all.

(*2 Corinthians 4:17* NIV)

Adversity is one of life's inescapable experiences, and it is difficult for us to be happy when it affects us personally. A popular theology says, "Just trust God and think rightly; then you won't have hardship." In searching the scriptures, however, we see that God has advanced His greatest servants through adversity, not prosperity.

God is not interested in making a generation of faint-hearted Christians. Instead, He uses trials to train up stalwart, spirit-filled soldiers for Jesus

Christ. Most of us don't even want to hear about difficulties, but it is far better to learn about adversity before you experience it than to face a hardship and wonder, *Lord, what on earth are You doing?*

We live in a fallen world, so like it or not, sin and its consequences surround us. Hardship is a part of life; it can cause discouragement and even despair, sometimes to the point of disillusionment. When we encounter such difficulty, we typically consider the ordeal unfair, unbelievable, and unbearable. Our attitude is usually, "It's not fair, God." But we should be asking, "What is God's point of view?"

If we experience no persecution or trials—if we have everything we want and none of the problems—what would we know about our heavenly Father? Our view of Him would be unscriptural and completely out of balance. Without adversity, we would never understand who God is or what He is like. God proves His faithfulness and He allows some situations from which He must rescue us.

Do you want the kind of faith that is based only on what you have heard or read? It is never *your* truth until God works it into your life. Most of us memorized these words before we even understood their meaning: "Yea, though I walk through the valley of the shadow of death, I will fear no evil: for Thou art with me" (v. 4). However, Psalm 23 doesn't become a living reality until we find ourselves in the valley.

Adversity can be a deadly discouragement, or God's greatest tool for advancing spiritual growth. Your response will make all the difference. Remember that God has a purpose for the hardship He has allowed, and it fits with His wonderful plan for your life.

PRAYER

There have been times in my life, Lord, when I have questioned my suffering, when I have cried out, "Why, Lord?" and there was no reply.

And yet You have encouraged me by allowing trials and suffering, drawing me to Yourself. You have withheld explanations I may not have been ready for. The hurt was real, but You have been an unforgettable comfort to me during those trying times. Though You did not author suffering, You can turn it around, giving it new meaning and purpose. Therefore, I thank You for it. Amen.

JOURNAL

_____

_____

_____

_____

_____

_____

_____

_____

_____

The Power of Love

But the greatest of these is love.
(1 Corinthians 13:13)

Nothing rivals the power of love. It heals, restores, mends, and makes all things new. Love surpasses all other virtues. The thirteenth chapter of First Corinthians tells us exactly what love is.

Love is "patient." It is never in a rush, never forceful, never demanding. It waits for God's best, whenever and whatever that may be. It refuses to yield to panic or grasp at temporal solutions.

Love is "kind." It acts in the best interest of others. It overlooks offenses. It is extravagant, giving more than what is asked or needed. Love "does not envy, it does not boast, it is not proud." It waits for God to promote and exalt. It credits Him for the success and acknowledges the contributions of others. It applauds the gain of another. It does not flaunt or taunt, but bends its knee in humility.

Love is not "rude." It is polite and courteous to all, even to those who are ill-mannered or ill-tempered. Love is not "self-seeking." It does not relentlessly pursue personal perfection, but gives priority to the kingdom of God.

Love "is not easily angered and keeps no record of wrongs." It is not irritated by the behavior of others. It refuses to judge, leaving that to God. It does not keep a mental record of offenses. Love does not delight in evil, but rejoices with the truth. It meets each day with cheer and a smile. It thinks upon good things and is happy in simple obedience to God.

Paul concludes this passage by saying that "love never fails." Not only does this indicate that love will never run out; it also means that

whatever the situation, the proper response
always is love. Responding with love keeps us
free—we are not imprisoned by bitterness, anger,
hostility, or an unforgiving spirit.

You can live in the shackles of hatred,
depression, and resentment, or you can be free—
the choice is yours. God is waiting to lead you
into an abundant life, redeemed by His love.

PRAYER

*Father, I want to be free! Free to love and be
loved. Please continue to teach me about the
wonder of Your love for me. Show me how to
accept it and then use me to demonstrate it
to others. God, I love You and thank You for
loving me first. Amen.*

JOURNAL

Conclusion

The abundant Christian life is based on God loving you and you being able to sense that love, to accept and experience it. Once you understand and enter into the unconditional love of God, which He offers regardless of what we have or have not done, you can't stop Him from loving you. You may be thinking, "Well, having done what I have done in life, and where I have been, how could God love me?" My friend, that is not the issue. The question you must answer is, can you accept His love?

Jesus made Himself very vulnerable. He was hurt, He felt pain, but He kept on loving. Did He stop loving Judas with his traitor's kiss in the garden? He did not. He loved Judas unconditionally—betrayal or not. So how does God want us to live? He wants you and me to be able to live with a sense of vulnerability—that we love people no matter what. Mark this down, you are going to be hurt, you will be disappointed, and you are going to be rejected at times. But are you willing to shut out what real love is all about? If you have ever had a taste of genuine, unconditional love, you know it is worth the risk. It is worth the chance of being rejected. How many times? Well, it just depends on how well you have been able to receive true love.

Sadly, many people are going to live and die never having experienced the power of genuine, unconditional love. No amount of material possessions, other relationships, exotic places to visit, prestige, prominence, prosperity, position, or power can match the awesome sense of the depth of fulfillment of experiencing unconditional love.

It is my prayer that over the last thirty-one days you have begun a new journey in experiencing the awesome power of God's love. Make praying, reading, and the study of God's word a priority in your daily life. Then you will experience life at its best—daily walking in the power of His unconditional love.

THE POWER OF LOVE

Have You Accepted God's Greatest Gift?

Our heavenly Father has prepared many special gifts and blessings for His children, but the greatest is the gift of eternal life though His Son Jesus. If you have never invited Him to be your Savior and Lord, you can right now by praying this simple prayer:

"Father, I know that I am a sinner. I believe Jesus died on the cross for my sins and paid my sin debt in full. Forgive me for my sins, and cleanse me of my past failures and guilt. I surrender control of my life to You today. Make me the person You have designed me to be. I pray this in Jesus' name. Amen."

If you sincerely prayed this to God, then according to God's Word, you have been

born again! I want to challenge you to take
positive steps to grow in your new faith.
Visit www.charlesstanleyinstitute.com and get
involved in our study program. Also, tell someone of your decision to follow Jesus and find
a church that will teach the uncompromised
truth of God's Word. Today is the first day on
a journey that will someday lead you into the
presence of your heavenly Father who has loved
you from the beginning of time.

Appendix

— DAY ONE —

We have come to know and have believed the love which God has for us. God is love, and the one who abides in love abides in God, and God abides in him. (1 John 4:16)

— DAY TWO —

The one who does not love does not know God, for God is love. (1 John 4:8)

The LORD is near to the brokenhearted and saves those who are crushed in Spirit. (Psalm 34:18)

— DAY THREE —

He will not cry out or raise His voice, nor make His voice heard in the street. A bruised reed He will not break and a dimly burning wick He will not extinguish. (Isaiah 42:2-3a)

— DAY FOUR —

We have thought on Your lovingkindness,
O God, in the midst of Your temple. (Psalm 48:9)

Never will I leave you; never will I forsake you.
(Hebrews 13:5b NIV)

For the king trusts in the LORD, and through the lovingkindness of the Most High he will not be shaken. (Psalm 21:7)

Satisfy us in the morning with your unfailing love, that we may sing for joy and be glad all our days.
(Psalm 90:14 NIV)

— DAY FIVE —

For His lovingkindness is great toward us.
(Psalm 117:2a)

For God so loved the world, that He gave His only begotten Son, that whoever believes in Him shall not perish, but have eternal life. (John 3:16)

Just as the Father has loved Me, I have also loved you; abide in My love. (John 15:9)

— DAY SIX —

Therefore, since we have been justified through faith, we have peace with God through our Lord Jesus Christ, through whom we have gained access by faith into this grace in which we now stand. (Romans 5:1-2a NIV)

For by grace you have been saved through faith; and that not of yourselves, it is the gift of God; not as a result of works, so that no one may boast. (Ephesians 2:8-9)

— DAY SEVEN —

This is love: not that we loved God, but that he loved us and sent his Son as an atoning sacrifice for our sins. (1 John 4:10 NIV)

Every good thing given and every perfect gift is from above, coming down from the Father of lights, with whom there is no variation or shifting shadow. (James 1:17)

— DAY EIGHT —

But love your enemies, do good to them. (Luke 6:35a NIV)

Do not repay evil with evil or insult with insult, but with blessing. (1 Peter 3:9a NIV)

. . . He did not retaliate; when he suffered, he made no threats. Instead, he entrusted himself to him who judges justly. (1 Peter 2:23 NIV)

— DAY NINE —

Man looks at the outward appearance, but the
LORD looks at the heart. (1 Samuel 16:7b)

— DAY TEN —

Though your sins are like scarlet, they shall be as
white as snow; though they are red as crimson, they
shall be like wool. (Isaiah 1:18b NIV)

— DAY ELEVEN —

My times are in Your hand. (Psalm 31:15a)

Going a little farther, he fell with his face to the
ground and prayed, "My Father, if it is possible,
may this cup be taken from me. Yet not as I will,
but as you will." (Matthew 26:39 NIV)

"For I know the plans I have for you," declares
the LORD, "plans to prosper you and not to harm
you, plans to give you a hope and a future."
(Jeremiah 29:11 NIV)

— DAY TWELVE —

Being confident of this, that he who began a good work in you will carry it on to completion until the day of Christ Jesus. (Philippians 1:6 NIV)

Do everything without complaining or arguing. (Philippians 2:14 NIV)

For it is God who works in you to will and to act according to his good purpose. (Philippians 2:13 NIV)

— DAY THIRTEEN —

Therefore as you have received Christ Jesus the Lord, so walk in Him. (Colossians 2:6)

For we walk by faith, not by sight. (2 Corinthians 5:7)

— DAY FOURTEEN —

Yet I hold this against you: You have forsaken your first love. (Revelation 2:4 NIV)

— DAY FIFTEEN —

[Paul] traveled through that area, speaking many words of encouragement to the people . . . (Acts 20:2a NIV)

Pleasant words are a honeycomb, sweet to the soul and healing to the bones. (Proverbs 16:24)

[Build] others up according to their needs, that it may benefit those who listen. (Ephesians 4:29b NIV)

— DAY SIXTEEN —

May the Lord direct your hearts into God's love. (2 Thessalonians 3:5a NIV)

— DAY SEVENTEEN —

Dear children, let us not love with words or tongue but with actions and in truth. (1 John 3:18 NIV)

For we are God's workmanship, created in Christ Jesus to do good works. (Ephesians 2:10a NIV)

— DAY EIGHTEEN —

I will bow down toward your holy temple and will praise your name for your love and your faithfulness. (Psalm 138:2a NIV)

Praise him for his acts of power. (Psalm 150:2a NIV)

Though the olive crop fails and the fields produce no food, though there are no sheep in the pen and no cattle in the stalls, yet I will rejoice in the LORD, *I will be joyful in God my Savior.* (Habakkuk 3:17b-18 NIV)

— DAY NINETEEN —

No one will snatch them out of My hand. (John 10:28b)

Love the Lord your God with all your heart and with all your soul and with all your strength. (Deuteronomy 6:5 NIV)

Your right hand upholds me. (Psalm 63:8)

*For I am the LORD, your God, who takes hold of
your right hand and says to you, Do not fear;
I will help you.* (Isaiah 41:13 NIV)

— DAY TWENTY —

For God loves a cheerful giver. (2 Corinthians 9:7b)

*For God so loved the world that he gave his one
and only Son.* (John 3:16a NIV)

*I live by faith in the Son of God, who loved me and
gave himself for me.* (Galatians 2:20b NIV)

*A generous man will prosper; he who refreshes
others will himself be refreshed.* (Proverbs 11:25 NIV)

Give, and it will be given to you. (Luke 6:38a)

— DAY TWENTY-ONE —

For Christ's love compels us. (2 Corinthians 5:14a NIV)

— DAY TWENTY-TWO —

For your lovingkindness toward me is great.
(Psalm 86:13a)

But as many as received Him, to them He gave the right to become children of God, even to those who believe in His name. (John 1:12)

— DAY TWENTY-THREE —

There is no fear in love. But perfect love drives out fear. (1 John 4:18a NIV)

I will ask the Father, and He will give you another Helper . . . that is the Spirit of truth, whom the world cannot receive, because it does not see Him or know Him, but you know Him because He abides with you and will be in you. I will not leave you as orphans; I will come to you. (John 14:16-18)

— DAY TWENTY-FOUR —

Those whom I love I rebuke and discipline.
(Revelation 3:19a NIV)

The Lord disciplines those he loves. (Hebrews 12:6a NIV)

Endure hardship as discipline; God is treating you as sons. (Hebrews 12:7a NIV)

God disciplines us for our good, that we may share in his holiness. (Hebrews 12:10b NIV)

— DAY TWENTY-FIVE —

. . . He has given us his very great and precious promises. (2 Peter 1:4a NIV)

You are the God who performs miracles; you display your power among the peoples. (Psalm 77:14 NIV)

Give, and it will be given to you. (Luke 6:38a)

— DAY TWENTY-SIX —

So Jacob served seven years to get Rachel, but they seemed like only a few days to him because of his love for her. (Genesis 29:20 NIV)

— DAY TWENTY-SEVEN —

But godliness actually is a means of great gain when accompanied by contentment. (1 Timothy 6:6)

. . . Every man who eats and drinks sees good in all his labor—it is the gift of God. (Ecclesiastes 3:13)

This is good, and pleases God our Savior, who wants all men to be saved and to come to a knowledge of the truth. (1 Timothy 2:3-4 NIV)

— DAY TWENTY-EIGHT —

Be kind and compassionate to one another, forgiving each other just as in Christ God forgave you. (Ephesians 4:32 NIV)

— DAY TWENTY-NINE —

I love the LORD, for he heard my voice; he heard my cry for mercy. Because he turned his ear to me, I will call on him as long as I live. (Psalm 116:1-2 NIV)

— DAY THIRTY —

For our light and momentary troubles are achieving for us an eternal glory that far outweighs them all. (2 Corinthians 4:17 NIV)

— DAY THIRTY-ONE —

But the greatest of these is love. (1 Corinthians 13:13b)

Transformation Journal

Use these pages to record how God has changed your understanding of genuine love.

_____

_____

_____

_____

_____

_____

_____

_____

_____

_____

_____

_____

_____

_____

_____

_____